Let it be HOT!

The story and philosophy

Kim
Permite Picante

Let it be HOT!

The story and philosophy

Terry Christopherson

ISBN 0-9666898-0-1

iff, Inc.
10 El Camino Real, 2nd Floor
San Carlos, CA 94070

TABLE OF CONTENTS

FOREWORD

This is a book written by a man who stopped long enough to face the underlying questions in the journey of his life. In it, the reader is challenged to take stock by honestly confronting the priorities, the motives, and the goals in his own life.

In a society that is racing ahead without a moment to spare, one can be pushed along without ever finding his footing. So many are being swept through life with no thought to their direction or their destination. Success is measured in dollar signs and bar graphs rather than on those things that make people human. Individuals everywhere are striving to accomplish that next rung on the ladder, in hopes that it will lead them a bit closer to happiness, to fulfillment, to success. One must scrutinize what his value subsists of before he has climbed to the sky only to find an even greater expanse of emptiness. Christopherson uses his own experience to hold up a mirror to his readers that they too might reflect on those things that really make them who they are. He draws on his extensive background in interpersonal relationships and personal management to illustrate the principles he has learned. The reader is prompted to strip away the surface elements of his life and realize his intrinsic value.

He is also called to take control of his attitude rather than allow his attitude to take control of him. Christopherson addresses problems such as guilt and poor self-esteem which keep people from making the most of their lives, and stirs the reader to combat such obstacles. Christopherson expresses that one needs a foundation on which to stand, and something in which to place his security, and encourages him to take hold of the time he is given that he may live life, not just watch it go by.

The ideas that Christopherson has to impart emerge through an illusory tale of a man in search of his own treasure. The reader is taken along on the character's arduous journey and allowed to observe his struggles and the lessons he learns along the way. By using the device of storytelling, Christopherson vividly portrays how one has the ability to manage his own life.

For the individual who is unsure of where he is headed, or even of what his purpose in life is, this book is a wonderful tool. It can be used to rouse the feelings and thoughts that lie at the core of one's person, so that he can contemplate who he is, why he is, and where he should be taking his life.

THE STORY

CHAPTER ONE

It was cold—the cold that comes to the desert at night after a long, hot day—the cold that comes as welcome relief from the scorching heat—the cold that creeps inside and chills to the bone.

He had forgotten the heat of the day, and the night chill reminded him of the long trek that had failed to reach the end of the high desert. The Sangre de Christo mountains loomed in the distance, appearing as far away then, at night, as they had that morning. All alone, the night would pass slowly for him. It's not really fear, but an uncertainty that grows as you peer into the blackness, looking for the unknown, hoping you don't see it.

One's mind begins to wander when influenced by extremes in temperature and fed only by the ache of fatigue and the uncertainty that a night without shelter can bring. Was that flicker up ahead just a mirage, or the inviting light of a warm campfire?

Each step closer to the light brought reassurance that it was welcome relief from the day's journey and the cold and loneliness of the night. The uncertainty of being alone was gradually replaced by the anxiety of meeting an unknown camper.

There was a lone figure sitting next to a fire, tending to a black cast-iron pot. The only other signs of life were a golden-colored dog curled up beside the fire, and a black mule grazing peacefully nearby.

The dog lifted his head, sniffing to evaluate the intentions of the approaching unexpected visitor. The mule, interested in making a meal of the sparse brush, only turned an ear to listen.

The explorer was now close enough to make out flickering details. The man by the black pot looked up, then stood and shielded his eyes to better see his new but unanticipated companion.

The man was old—the old that life brings—old in wisdom and experience—not the old of frailty, but of strength. His clothes were worn, not tattered. The twinkle in his eye and faint smile through his gray beard sent a warm invitation. The apprehension was fading.

The explorer's discomfort from both the long day and the chance meeting began to leave, and was replaced by the anticipation of rest and conversation. Without a word, he was directed to sit and warm. A friendly glance and a brief "My name's Jed, how about a bowl of red?" meant dinner was served.

He was handed a bowl made of sky blue pottery, the kind seen at many of the local pueblos. It was old, not cracked or chipped, but old with the character that age brings to all things. It was filled with a thick red, the color of the iron red plateaus at sunset—chili. The bowl was fiery from the chili's heat, and steam rose from its surface into the night air. It felt good to wrap his cold fingers around its sides and feel his blood begin to flow once again.

With the security of the fire and some amount of comfort beginning to return, the explorer realized how hungry he was. With the night air quickly cooling the chili to a suitable temperature for eating, he eagerly took the first bite.

The cook could not hold back a smile as his guest gasped from the fire that comes from chilies grown, dried, and aged in the mountains of New Mexico. He felt a touch of sympathy as he caught the widened, almost desperate look in his visitor's eyes, and saw the beads of sweat breaking out on his forehead, glistening in the firelight.

Handing him a canteen of water, the old man gently said, "Let it be hot."

The explorer grabbed the canteen and frantically took a long drink. The canteen dropped from his burning lips. The water had not quenched the fire; his eyes still held their look of shock, but it was now mixed with that of disbelief.

The old man repeated, but this time with more command in his tone, "Let it be hot! The secret to eating chilies is to let them be hot. Quit trying to fight the heat. Just let it be hot."

It was only hunger that motivated the second bite. Trying hard to relax and not fight the heat, he found that the second, much smaller bite was hot, but not as bad as the first. The beads of sweat still broke out, but this time, the flavor of the chili was there, not just the heat.

Satisfaction, even a pleasant sensation, filled his body, and a strange desire for more chili replaced the desire to grab for the canteen.

When the blue bowl had been emptied, the water tasted almost sweet; a welcome thirst-quenching beverage, not a frantic attempt to put out the fire.

CHAPTER TWO

Sitting back to relax, the old man began to speak. "To enjoy chilies, you must learn not to fight the heat. Try to resist that first impulse of tightening every muscle, hoping by force not to let the chili burn. The chili is hot; you must accept that. Nothing you can do will keep it from being hot. Not water, not *cerveza*, nothing. You have the choice to go beyond the heat and experience the subtle flavors. Go beyond the heat to a point of even enjoying the heat.

"Chilies are so much like life's pressures and conflicts. To succeed in life you must remember to 'let it be hot' when confronted with crisis and trial. Our first response when conflict and pressure come is a combination of resistance and fear. The chili is hot; resistance and fear will not change that. Sooo... 'LET IT BE HOT!!!'"

"Fighting that first impulse is the first step in overcoming whatever life dishes out. So relax and allow the heat to be there. You will avoid doing something you will regret later. By just 'letting it be hot', you are ahead, in that you do not make things worse. 'Let it be hot'... Your first impulse tends to stir up the heat instead of looking for a solution."

After stirring the fire, which sent a cascade of sparks into the night sky, the old man sat back quietly. In the light of the brightened flames, his face showed the wisdom of solitude and contemplation. He watched the sparks rise into the clear night sky and mingle undistinguished with the stars, then he continued:

"The chili is not hot out of meanness, it's just hot. The pressures and attacks that come at us are not mean, even when the one attacking is motivated by meanness. To confuse the attack itself with the meanness of the attacker only clouds our thinking and causes us to respond to the person attacking instead of dealing with the situation. 'Let it be hot;' resist the first impulse to lash out against the person. It is not the person you must deal with, it is the attack you must diffuse before finding a solution."

"Life is hard, you know, it's just hard. Some heat we bring on ourselves, some comes from others with misguided motives, and some pressure is just part of living. To try pushing the heat away is to fight a battle that cannot be won. 'Let it be hot!' It is not the absence of heat that makes a life successful; it is the ability to cope with the heat that makes us successful."

The stars seemed close enough to touch. The explorer lay by the fire considering the meal and the advice he had just received. He realized that his new friend was more than a cook, he was a bit of a philosopher as well. The dog moved closer to investigate and lay down next to the explorer, who knew he was now accepted. As he reached out to pet him, the dog wagged his tail.

He felt so far away from his life. His life, like the stars, was still out there somewhere, but out of reach here in the high desert. How much of his life he had spent fighting the heat! He had enjoyed many things, and had his share of pain—pretty average, he supposed—and that was the problem.

This was the first time he had set out on his own, and until tonight, even this was turning out like so many plans in the past: a great beginning followed by long stretches of boredom—a bold start leading to a disrupted journey, disrupted due to a lack of direction and motivation.

In the past he had spent his time either fighting or avoiding anything that was difficult. The idea that he could be in control and find a solution in any situation was both comforting and frustrating. To think how many opportunities he had missed...

The moon rose, silhouetting the Sangre de Christos. He drifted off to sleep knowing that lost chances were gone and best forgotten. His last thought was the anticipation of tomorrow mixed with a little uncertainty, and a fresh determination to press on.

CHAPTER THREE

The first light of morning is a celebration of life's constant cycles. The birds know it best—they sing more beautifully in the cool of dawn. Their music of optimism proclaims a belief that today will be a better day.

The *Sangre de Christo* mountains seemed a little closer, though still at a distance that challenged the explorer's optimism. A good night's sleep by the fire had eased his tired muscles and refreshed his mind.

They packed and began walking. Neither one talked for quite some time. The companionship was welcome, even with the question of how he had ended up with a traveling partner still unanswered.

The dog led the way, somehow knowing where they were headed. The old man, Jed, walked silently alongside the explorer while leading the mule. Last night played heavily on the explorer's mind. "Let it be hot." It did seem to take some of the fire from the bowl of chili, but why? The chili had not changed, only his reaction to it had. Yet, what a difference that had made.

The sun was well above the mountains before either man spoke.

"Jed, why does it work?"

As if he were anticipating the question, Jed began to speak, "Remember, in any situation there is only one thing you have complete control over, and that is your attitude—how you think and what you think. You have the choice to see the worst or the best, the choice to react or respond, the choice to be positive or negative, the choice to complain or look for solutions."

"One great truth of the ages is that our attitude either makes a situation worse or better, depending on whether it is positive or negative. The secret, then, is that by controlling how we think, how we see, we are able to influence everything that comes into our life, even if that control only governs how we will allow life to affect us."

"When you 'let it be hot,' you took away much of the chili's ability to burn. As with most difficulties, resistance intensifies the 'heat;' so it is with hot food. The spice may be intense, but your attitude governs how it will affect you."

The sun climbed higher in the sky, changing the colors of the plateaus and mountains as it went, turning up the heat of the day. The explorer began to feel resentment toward the hot sun. Could 'let it be hot' take away some of the sun's power as well?

CHAPTER FOUR

The dry creek bed which they had followed most of the day took a sudden turn to the north, then disappeared. Jed stopped the mule and knelt down near the spot where the creek bed came to an end. Moving aside a large rock, he uncovered a small pool of water.

"Let's rest here," Jed said quietly, reaching for a canteen to fill from the pool. Jed handed him the canteen, and he took a long drink. The water was cold and sweet—must have come from deep in the ground. It was the most quenching drink he could remember.

The sun was hot, but they found minor relief in the shade of a dead tree and some rocks near the edge of the stream. From somewhere in his bag, Jed produced pieces of jerky seasoned with a pepper that brought back memories of the night before.

As they ate, more questions filled the explorer's mind. "I suppose you're right, but where does one's attitude come from, and how do we gain control?"

Jed had endless patience and began to explain, "Your reaction to the chili came from how you expected the chili to taste and from what you thought would make the heat go away. When you let it be hot, you took control of your attitude, changed your expectations, and realized that what had worked in the past would not necessarily work every time."

"Your attitude sits on a foundation of self worth and faith. Our value comes not from what we do, but from who we are, from who made us. We have value because we were formed in the very 'image of God', and for that reason alone, we have value. Values are what we hold dear. Self worth is the measure of how dear we hold our-selves. Knowing you have value and values gives you the strength and courage to let it be hot."

"Faith is having a conviction that our values are not only true, but can be counted on. Faith has to have an object. You don't just 'have faith', you have faith in some-thing. 'Let it be hot' worked because you had the faith to try."

"There are many truths that will only affect our lives when we have the faith to test them. Truth is absolute. It is true whether we recognize it or act upon it. Faith is the catalyst that puts truth into action. Faith does not make it true, faith makes it work."

CHAPTER FIVE

The shade of the old tree enticed them to linger in the relative cool. It did seem that in not fighting the sun, its intensity was diminished.

"If self worth is the foundation of attitude, then how does one build that sense of value?" the explorer asked.

"It all starts with how you see yourself, your self image," Jed began. "Most of our life, we look into the mirror of others' comments and form a picture of what we think we are like. The more important the person is in our life, the more credibility we give him. That is why parents have such an important responsibility."

"Most people have an inaccurate picture: we emphasize the negative and discount the positive. We hear the criticism of others and internalize it while ignoring the positive. The result is an out-of-focus picture of who we are and what we can do."

"To begin realizing our self worth, we must first deal with the image we hold. We must take an accurate look and realize that there are flaws, even areas that are wrong, yet, the positive qualities are many. We have value because of who we are, not what we do. Remember, our value comes from who made us."

Jed paused to let this all sink in, but it was clear he had more to say. After a few moments, he continued, "This knowledge of self worth leads to humility rather than arrogance. Genuine humility and pride go together. False humility and debasing are just the other side of arrogance. Our awareness of value influences not only how we treat ourselves, but how we treat others, and how we respond in any situation. The knowledge of your value allows you to look for the best in any circumstance because you are freed from looking on every negative as a threat to your value."

The explorer thought about how he had pursued accomplishment out of a feeling that if he only did enough, he could feel better about himself. In all his success, he never felt it was enough, and he usually focused on his failures.

CHAPTER SIX

"It's a long way from any city out here. Where are you headed?" Jed asked as they started up again.

The explorer felt confident enough to tell Jed the circumstances that had brought them together. "Gold."

"Gold?"

"Many years ago a great aunt of mine received a letter from an Indian friend who had stumbled on a vein of gold quartz. He had carried out two fist-size chunks and had them assayed in Taos. They proved to be high in gold content. In his letter, the Indian described the landmarks and drew a rough sketch of where he had found the gold, but he was never able to return. The letter has passed through two generations and was given to me in a bundle of other keepsakes. The description seemed so clear that I decided to set out in search of the treasure."

Jed was silent for a bit, then spoke, "The search for treasure has led many to the *Sangre de Christo*. I hope you find what you seek."

The explorer was relieved that Jed had neither ridiculed him, nor asked to see the letter. They walked on in silence for some time. As the sun approached the horizon, Jed stopped by a spring near an out-cropping of rock: a strange, almost out of place formation that pointed up into the air and leaned toward the mountains, as if giving directions. The explorer recognized its shape and size as one of the landmarks in his letter. His heart beat faster, but, he kept his thoughts to himself.

They quenched their thirst at the spring and then prepared to spend another night.

CHAPTER SEVEN

As the sun slipped below the mountains, the explorer noticed that although they had traveled many miles that day, the mountains seemed no closer. As if reading his mind, Jed began, "A goal is a funny thing. We design a destination and set out, the path laid out clearly in our mind. Yet, as we journey, the goal that was so clear changes shape so much that it often bears no resemblance to our original vision. In the end, it is the direction that is most important. The destination usually takes care of itself.

Success is a journey, not a destination. More often than not, our goals are limiting, not large enough, and not what we really want. But as we travel toward a dream, heading in a direction that is right, we begin to see goals that match our wants. Those goals are attainable, believable, and fulfilling.

"The distance to the mountains is hard to estimate. Distance and time are deceiving, yet all of a sudden, you will find you are there. By tomorrow night you will probably be at your destination. I hope you find what you are seeking."

CHAPTER EIGHT

The sun playing on the distant mountains created a palette of iron oxide and burnt ochre. The changing colors hypnotized the explorer, intensifying the inner searching he was experiencing. He had a new sensation of strength. Though Jed was actually leading, the explorer felt a growing confidence even in these unfamiliar surroundings. His first response had been that to "let it be hot" would make him passive, but instead, it gave him a sense of control over the sun itself. Control over attitude was giving him control over the other forces in his life, and a feeling of strength and confidence.

The start of his journey seemed so far away. Setting out in search of riches creates an exciting kind of euphoria. He had done little planning and had packed too little. He had told few where he was going—no one knew all the details. The desert sun and Jed had changed his focus. The mountains still loomed and drew him, yet the desire for treasure was a bit subdued. He was surprised by how he had come face to face with life. He was finding answers to questions he had never really thought to ask, but had been searching for for years.

Jed was busy building a fire as the sun slipped below the horizon. The explorer made several trips collecting wood enough to last through the night. The intense heat of the day would soon be gone, making the fire's heat welcome.

CHAPTER NINE

Jed placed a handful of dark earth-red dried chilies in one of the blue ceramic bowls, and covered them with water. There were large chilies and a few small ones. Jed's explanation was that they had "different flavors and different heat," the smaller chilies being hotter. There was probably some lesson there, but he let it go for now.

The explorer walked over to the fire and recognized the black pot from the night before. Another pot of chili was on the menu. Inside the pot, garlic and onion cooked slowly in oil. Jed was chopping the now soft chilies, and dicing chunks of beef. When the onions and garlic were tender, he added the chilies and beef along with cumin, oregano, salt, and pepper. Then, to the explorer's surprise, from somewhere in the pack, Jed produced a bottle of *cerveza*. Jed opened the bottle and poured its contents into the pot, refilled the bottle at the spring, and poured in the water. He stirred the mixture with a long wooden spoon, then sat back to watch.

"Be ready in a while," Jed said quietly. The explorer knew another lesson was coming. "Funny thing about a pot of chili— always good, never quite the same. Depends on the peppers, mostly. It's an awful lot like a journey— you know the general result you have in mind, but the details that come along the way aren't clear at the start. There are times we know exactly where we wish to end up, and we have only to lay out a path to get there. But more often, we know the general direction, and the final destination becomes clear along the way."

Jed would pause occasionally to stir the black pot of chili. As it cooked, the aroma filled the air. When he sat back down, he continued. "A lot of folks never even get started because they don't know where they want to end up. Better to start, head in the right direction, and know that the details will become clear as you go."

"Others are so afraid of failure that they never even start. 'Better not to try than to try but fail' is their motto. It's worse to never try than to try and not succeed. Success is a journey, not a destination."

The explorer was all too aware of how fear and uncertainty had held him back. Most of his friends saw his current adventure as out of character for him. He had enjoyed today; the day was memorable not from it's end, but from the journey itself.

CHAPTER TEN

Night approached quickly, and with it, the explorer's anticipation of another bowl of red. The dog assumed his position near the fire, and the donkey wandered lazily nearby. The black pot simmered, and that wonderful aroma stimulated the explorer's appetite.

Jed asked quietly, "Still looking to find that treasure?"

For the first time, the explorer realized that he had not even thought about gold all day.

"Well, Jed, to tell the truth, I haven't given it a thought today. Most days, I am filled with an urgency, a restlessness, but not today. About all I've thought about today is what you said about attitude. Funny thing—you told me to 'let it be hot' and the chili would lose its heat. Today as we walked in the sun, I tried that with the afternoon heat, and it seemed to help."

Jed just smiled.

"Jed, it so often seems that we have little control in our life. Today I found that I could control how I thought, something that I must say, is new. Most of my life I've been searching, looking for something that would bring contentment. Guess I never really knew what I wanted.

One thing I do know: my direction and desires both floated with the wind. Jed, do you ever wonder if it really matters where we end up?"

"The real problem," Jed began, "is that we never know when we'll reach the end or what it will be like when we do. Right now, we are heading for those mountains, but neither one of us is sure just where on the mountains we will end up—can't tell that until we are closer. Then, once we are there, will we stop, or keep on? Seems to me that the direction is more important than the destination. If we head in the right direction, the final destination will become clear as we get close to it and we will find out that we ended up okay."

Jed continued, "One thing I do know is that we have more control over what we think than where we go. When you control your mind, you will then find that your journey and dreams will follow. The reason you have 'floated with the wind' is that you allowed outside forces to mold your thinking. When you 'let it be hot', you control your thinking, and the result is that you gain more control of your direction."

CHAPTER ELEVEN

The black pot had simmered and bubbled for about an hour when Jed finally proclaimed it ready. Jed filled two blue bowls and handed one to his traveling companion. The cold night air, the smell, the heat of the bowl, and the explorer's hunger all came to a climax, and he quickly took the first bite. The chili was as hot as before, but what a difference. With the admonition to 'let it be hot' fresh on his mind, he savored the flavor and found the spice a compliment, not an irritant. He was able to stay in control and resist the urges to fight the heat.

What a change; just a day earlier, black pepper had been the extent of *picante* in his diet, and now he was enjoying fiery food. A day earlier, he had thought of little but his nowhere life and dreamt of instant riches. Now the riches seemed less urgent, and direction, more important. His daily problems that had so overwhelmed him before, were more manageable now that he had control of his attitude toward them. All of this from "a bowl of red?"

A shooting star streaked across the sky, and a smile came to the explorer's face. He had no idea what the future held for him but didn't care, he would deal with it with confidence and control, and look for the positive. Even the mountains looked a little more friendly.

CHAPTER TWELVE

The sun, again, rose bright in the eastern sky, silhouetting the mountains that had moved closer in the night. The men got up quickly to take advantage of the cooler travel of morning. Jed's word's from last evening stirred in the explorer anticipation for the day.

"We should make the mountains by lunch time."

As they set out, the explorer found that the mountains did look reachable, and he wondered what they would find there. The mountains had been the destination that had started his adventure. That seemed so long ago. They had been the keeper of the treasure that he had been so sure would change his life. Now, as he neared his final destination, he was feeling that his life had already changed—that he was richer somehow, than when he had started.

As they packed, he detected a change in Jed, an air of anticipation. The golden dog and the donkey seemed to have a little more energy as well. The explorer realized that Jed never showed his feelings. There was a warmth that was immediately felt, but he never showed excitement or enthusiasm. He was methodical, never in a hurry, but not slow. Given a choice, one would always say Jed was positive, never negative. He had a quiet enthusiasm, one that the explorer sensed so subtly, that it took a change like this morning for him to ever consider Jed's outlook.

The change in energy affected the explorer, and his excitement for the day grew. Once again, the dog took the lead, and they started out. The morning passed without much conversation, and the ground began to incline. The desert plants were changing to mountain greenery, with trees and shadows to break the sun's heat. They started up a gentle draw, and Jed asked, "Excited?"

The explorer's only response was, "Yes, but not sure why or what to expect to find."

Jed reminded him, "Remember, 'let it be hot.' If you stay in control and follow the right path, the destination will become clear."

Another hundred yards, and the draw took a sharp turn to the south where it became much steeper. The explorer had led the way for the last half hour or so. He was concentrating on putting one foot ahead of the other, and had not spoken to Jed at all. The dog would wander off into the trees and be gone for quite some time, then show up as if he had been on a mission.

At last, they came out on top of a small plateau. The explorer dropped his pack and ran to the edge. The view was spectacular. He could see far out into the desert, the horizon lined with plateaus as far as he could see. He turned around to see how far ahead he was from the others, only to find that he was alone. From his vantage point, he could see all along the path he had taken, but there was no sign of Jed, the donkey, or the dog.

It wasn't really fear that overtook him, there was no fear that anything was wrong, but a strange questioning sensation that made him wonder if he had just imagined his companions, or if they had been real. Turning back to pick up his pack, he lost his breath at what he saw. There, sitting perched atop his pack, was a sky blue ceramic bowl, the very bowl that had held his first bowl of red.

He ran to every edge of the plateau, but there was no one in sight. As questions flooded his mind, he sat holding the bowl in his hands, and was reminded of the one lesson he had learned, "let it be hot." He forced himself to gain control of his thoughts, about where he was, and what had happened, and as he did, the fear and uncertainty faded and was replaced by a sense of confidence in his ability to deal with life.

CHAPTER THIRTEEN

Only one short week away, in retrospect, seemed like forever, but the explorer was now back to the life that had once been "normal." Things were so different now—clearly the result of changes in him, not his world. His mind drifted often to the desert and the *Sangre de Christo* mountains.

Those around him commented on the peace and confidence he showed. Yes, he had changed, and as a result, so had his world. The ringing of his cellular phone jolted him back to reality.

"Hello."

"Oh great, you're back! Well, did you find your treasure?" a familiar voice on the other end asked; the sarcasm was easily detected.

"You could say so," he responded. "Do you have time for lunch to hear about it?"

"Sure. Where?"

"I know a new place. Meet me there. It's called *Permite Picante.*"

"You never liked Mexican food before!"

"People change."

THE PHILOSOPHY

FACING QUESTIONS

Life is a journey. You have destinations to reach and routes to choose. Along the way there are obstacles and forks in the road. Our success depends on how we deal with those challenges. Ultimately, it is direction that makes the difference; destination will follow.

We must face some basic questions:

- Do I deserve to succeed?

- Why go at all?

- What do I have control of?

- Am I just a victim of fate?

- What is the source of passion and guidance?

Our answers to these questions will determine our contentment in the present and our destination in the future, for it is our answers to these questions that shape how we set our direction. Our life is the result of the choices we make along the journey; the why, the how, and the what of life is our compass. To avoid these issues is to be locked into aimless wandering; to answer inadequately is to head in a definite direction that leads to the wrong destination. All movement and all directions are not equal. Many have been sincere, but many are sincerely wrong.

WHY GO AT ALL?

On a recent flight, I met one of the most inspiring people I have ever had the chance to meet. She was returning from two months in Mexico and was as excited as a teenager to be getting back home to her husband. She is a beautiful woman in every way. She has a smile that can warm a room and an attitude that is contagious. She is an attorney and works with abused women and children. She's truly a success: successful career, successful marriage—she is a positive, satisfied person.

It was not always that way. We talked for twenty minutes before I found that she was almost completely deaf; her lip reading was highly developed. As a child, she was seriously abused. Her hearing loss was the result of blows to the ears. Her spine was broken so badly that even today doctors cannot believe that she walks. Yet, with all of the misfortune in her past, she has avoided bitterness and self pity.

I asked her how she had avoided the victim mentality.

"I was allowed to live, so I live each day to the fullest.... I realized that I deserved to have a good life."

It was the realization that God had some purpose for her life, that she had value, that formed the basis for a fulfilled and satisfied life.

To deserve is not the same as being worthy or perfect. Ask any parent who has a child who has gone astray. They will agree that the actions have made the child unworthy, but that the child is not worthless. Most parents would give all they have, even their own life, to redeem the wayward child and restore him. Any parent knows that whatever the child may have done, he is not worthless, just unworthy. The story of the prodigal son clearly expresses that Christ considered us valuable enough to redeem. In His eyes, we were lost, but valuable. Our value is not in what we have done, but in what we are: creatures created in God's image.

We tend to equate value with function or performance. Value comes not from what we do, but what we are. We are human, not machine, not merely another animal.

LOOK IN THE MIRROR

Put a mirror up to your face and take a look. See your hair, the way it is combed? Notice your jewelry, your makeup, even your clothing. Now focus on one feature of your face. I know what 60 —80% of the population focus on when they look into the mirror; they see a feature they don't like: eyes too big—too small, nose too large—too small, mouth too wide—too narrow, no chin—too many chins...

Question: Where did we get the idea that the feature is deficient? Most often it was from a comment that was made a long time ago, usually in our childhood by another child or an adult. Remember the rhyme? "Sticks and stones may break my bones, but names can never hurt me." It was a common salve to wounded feelings, but doesn't have an ounce of truth. Physical injuries heal, but names and labels are long term. Names and labels do more harm and hurt longer and deeper than any physical injury.

If our "mirror" only showed our exterior, it would be difficult enough, but it looks deep inside. In it, we see our strengths and weaknesses, our talents and failures. As with the physical, we tend toward the negative. We remember the failure and focus on the weakness. We draw the conclusion that since we are not perfect, we also have little value.

In the early 1980's, *Time* magazine named as their "Person of the Year" the computer. I remember being offended, even revolted, by their choice. We are not computers; we are humans.

That computer that they were so highly impressed with would be worthless junk today. When a machine can no longer perform, it has no value, and it is discarded.

Our value as human beings is not dependent on what we do, but on what we are—not on our function, but on who made us.

IT AFFECTS ALL

As children, we are taught that our acceptance is often dependent upon our performance. We are admonished to "be a good little girl." We are rewarded for our accomplishments but seldom "just because I love you."

How often we are compared to others: "why can't you be more like your brother?" Measuring up is prized, and value is conditioned on what we accomplish, on the awards we receive, on the grades we earn, and the people we impress—not on what we are.

I was conducting a seminar in Bellevue, Washington on conflict and emotion management. At lunch, I talked with a young woman who, according to the standards set by the media and advertising, "had it all." She was approximately 25 years old, was dressed well, was intelligent and beautiful. Most of the time we spoke, about 45 minutes, she had tears running down her face. She said, "I wish people would not tell me how beautiful I am. I wish they would look inside, but I am afraid that if they did, they would find out that I am really ugly."

The next day I was speaking on the same topic in a different city. A man approached me at lunch. I would guess he was 55–60 years old, his hands showed he had worked hard most of those years. He stood there fighting back tears and said, "My problem is that I hate myself inside."

Two different people in two different situations—the same result. Our age, appearance, or career have nothing to do with our awareness of value. If we determine our value based on what we do, not what we are, we will often feel valueless.

We all must realize that our value does not depend on what we do, but is the result of what we are. It is not a question of whether or not we have value, it is the recognition of our value.

***Self worth:* our awareness of our intrinsic value.**

NOT PERFECT, BUT WORTH
IMPROVING!

"Can a person have too much self worth?"

"No!"

Arrogance is an inflated view of yourself. You need to have an honest appraisal of yourself, not tearing down, not inflated.

Self worth is actually humbling, because you do not have to compare yourself to others. Arrogance is the result of a competition to see who is best. A person with an accurate self awareness knows that we all have value, that we all have abilities, that we are not all the same. Since our value is intrinsic, the need to declare our superiority is gone. Since we both have value, competition is meaningless; we both have won.

"If we are this valuable, does it follow that we are perfect?"

"No!"

Our value is not dependent on our perfection, but because we have value, we are worth improving. Guilt prevents us from being all we can be. Guilt leads to fear and anger, which are both devastating to our self esteem. It is only when the guilt is removed that we are truly able to appreciate our value.

A sign of low self esteem is to avoid, or even ridicule self improvement. Because of our value, we have a responsibility to be the best we can be. Secure that our value is separate from being perfect, admitting weakness or failure is no longer a threat. Knowing that we have value, we work to improve ourselves as a demonstration of our value.

YOU ALWAYS HAVE
CONTROL OF ONE THING

Our Creator has endowed us with many gifts, none so precious as the ability to choose how we think, that is, to choose our attitude.

Attitude: how we choose to think about, or view, any situation.

The choice of our attitude is the one and only thing that we will always have control of. Napoleon Hill observed that if attitude was our constant choice, then it must have tremendous value and power.

Attitude is a learned behavior. Dr. Martin Seligman found that by the age of nine or ten, our attitude is pretty well shaped, and that unless we consciously work to change our way of thinking, we carry our attitude through life.

The job of a parent or a teacher is much like that of a coach. Lou Holtz, one time coach for the Notre Dame football team, was asked how he motivated his players. He responded, "It's not my job to motivate them, they come to me motivated. It's my job to not de-motivate them." Children are born optimists. You would have to be an optimist just to be born. As we "train up a child" we must not tear him down. We must be vigilant in keeping and feeding their optimism.

Children learn about attitude by observing our way of dealing with everyday events. Negativity, criticism, catastrophising, and living in the past communicate that we assume the worst and are victims; pessimistic thinking in us results in pessimistic thinking in them. Looking for opportunities, learning from the past, then putting it behind us and moving on, expecting the best, and focusing on personal strengths, not weaknesses... such optimistic thinking in us results in optimistic thinking in our children.

Attitude control is more than just a habit; it is an expression of faith. To maintain a positive attitude without a foundation for that optimism is difficult and a bit unrealistic. Unless we hold a belief in a Grand Purpose, we have no basis for optimism. When serious trials come, we need more than the habit of optimism; we need the security of faith. We need the confidence that all events, even those we do not understand, work together for an ultimate goal. We need to know that life has meaning and is not merely a series of chance happenings.

Surrendering to a victim mentality, "I can do nothing; there is no hope," robs a person of joy and peace. It feeds the feeling of helplessness and hopelessness that leads to depression. Outside forces and other people may have the ability to harm, but how we face the situation is our choice. How we deal with both prosperity and hardship is both determined by, and a demonstration of, our faith.

To correct what Zig Ziglar calls, "Stinking Thinking," start focusing on the positive. Take more time to be thankful. Try keeping a notebook and entering in at least one thing you are thankful for each day.

Listen to your self-talk. Brian Tracey says, "77% of what we say to ourselves is negative." Tune your inner ear to be sensitive to negative self-talk and replace it with positive affirmations. The Bible says that the tongue is the hardest thing to control, and it tells us to avoid negative talk. That includes how you talk to yourself. Just as damage is done with unwholesome talk to others, so is damage done to our attitude when we talk ourselves down.

Surround yourself with positive people; their enthusiasm is contagious. Avoid complainers and criticizers, for they too are contagious.

Greet everyone with a smile. William James wrote, "The emotions are not always immediately responsive to intellect, but are always immediately responsive to action." Feelings follow action. If you begin to act like you you want to feel, the emotions will follow.

Remember, attitude is a learned habit. Begin acting as if a positive attitude is already yours, and the feeling will come. This is the essence of faith, acting as if something is true before we see it fulfilled.

FOLLOW YOUR DREAM

"I find the great thing in this world
is not so much where we stand, as in
what direction we are moving."
—Oliver Wendell Homes, Jr.

"How do I decide 'what I want to be when I grow up?'"

"Never grow up, but keep on growing in the right direction. Success is a journey, not a destination."

To dream, or to set goals is the question. On my tape Dare to Dream, I define a dream as, "that vision that leads us on and motivates us to do the things necessary for success." A goal defines the steps along the way. Set long term dreams and move toward them with short term goals.

Dreams vary. Some are more specific than others, most are general. When Robert Schuller set out to build the Crystal Cathedral, he had a vision of a magnificent building made of glass. As the project began to take shape, short term goals moved him closer and defined the final look of the cathedral.

The difference between a stagnant life and one that is productive is movement. Henry David Thoreau said, "If one advances in the direction of his dreams, one will meet with success unexpected in common hours." The right direction brings the right destination.

Moving in the right direction is living consistent with your values while pursuing your interests and talents. To do so demands that we define our values, explore our interests, and develop the talents we have been given.

Children come into the world with limitless interests, latent talents, and no values. They will learn values from what they see and from how they are treated. They will explore their interests and talents until they are discouraged from doing so. The fortunate are those who never stop exploring.

Many of us stopped taking the risks that a dream demands, and have had to learn again how to dream. We have been dulled by "responsibility" and "practicality." Fear of ridicule and low self esteem keep us from even trying anything new or different.

Children are natural artists. Most love to draw and paint, but, as Betty Edwards has observed in *Drawing on the Right Side of the Brain*, by the age of twelve to fourteen, most have given up and adopted the adult view of, "I can't draw." Edwards has been able to rekindle that early ability and teach most any adult to do a reasonable job of sketching. The good news is that we can, in fact, we must, learn again to be curious and try new activities.

In the movie *Shirley Valentine*, Shirley asks, "Why are we given all this life if we were never meant to live it?" She learns that we can live it; we can find childlike energy, curiosity, and confidence. We can dream again, and in so doing, begin to travel in the right direction—in so doing, begin to live this life we have been given.

VALUES:
A GUIDE FOR THE
PRESENT

What do you hold as true? What do you consider as absolute, the point at which you cannot compromise? What do you do when no one else is looking? What would you do if you would never be caught? What would you trust your life and future on? These are your values. We all have values; some just work better than others. For our values to be right, we must answer some basic questions and make sure that the values match reality.

Questions:

- Why am I here?

- What is my purpose?

- How do I determine right and wrong— a standard?

- What determines my future?

- How do you explain the human dilemma— good and evil?

Francis Schaeffer taught that to be true, our presuppositions must match reality. I may choose to adopt a belief or value system; that is a choice we all have. If that system answers the above questions and "works," that is, it gives answers and guidance in real day-to-day life, then it is the value system to trust. If it doesn't, then find another.

Does your value system pass? If not, you will find yourself in frequent conflict with decisions regarding right and wrong, as well as choices concerning priorities. If not, know that truth can be found. It is not our perception that creates truth, truth is true, we must accept and act upon the truth. The Bible says "The truth shall set you free."

VALUES AND THE FUTURE

Embracing the right values eliminates one of our biggest fears: "What does the future hold?" Fear of the future, or hopelessness, is crippling.

No one who saw the women's gymnastics in the 1996 Atlanta Olympics will ever forget Kerri Strug. With the competition in the balance, I watched with confidence as she prepared to take her first run at the vault. I was still confident as she completed a perfect vault only to land, injuring her ankle. The audience gasped, but I was not worried at all. She limped back to the starting line, the pain obvious. Announcers and fans watched her nervously to see if she would, or could, make another needed vault to capture the gold medal. Me? I was still calm, cool, and collected.

What she did next will go down in the history of sports and courage. I watched calmly as she ran down the runway, vaulted perfectly, and landed correctly, though in intense pain. The crowd was ecstatic, the media stunned, yet as amazing as it was to watch, I was not surprised.

You see, due to the time zone I was in, I was watching a delayed broadcast. I knew the USA would win; I just didn't know the details. I could stay calm even in the face of tragedy, because I knew how it would all turn out. The right values let you put today's setbacks in perspective, because you "know who is going to win."

Knowing the end, you can follow your dreams, because you have no fear of the final destiny. Truly, "the right direction brings the right destination."

INTERESTS

What do you like to do? Where does your mind wander when you are stuck in an activity you dislike? What has always brought you satisfaction? Are there issues that motivate or emotionally move you?

Dale Carnegie said, "There is only one way to get anybody to do anything; that is to make them want to do it." Carnegie was describing passion. What we like to do and what we want to do are closely related. When we pursue what we like or what we want, we are motivated. The bumper sticker says, "Work is for the people who don't know how to fish." We are passionate about what we are interested in, and will go out of our way to pursue it.

I was recently in Racine, Wisconsin. It was March (still winter). The hotel was next to a river which was partially frozen. The temperature outside was 10–20 degrees F, too cold for me. In the morning there were fishermen standing in the icy water fishing—they had a passion for fishing. The night before, I had overheard them as they talked about how they had traveled from far away for the sole purpose of standing in that frigid water with temperatures below freezing—they had a passion for fishing. What we like, we do with pleasure. Even unpleasant circumstances become bearable.

People who succeed are people who like what they do. Athletes, entertainers, and professionals who do well, do so for the love of the game or activity. Strong relationships and families work not as a result of duty, but as a natural extension of pursuing common interests and values. Passion comes first, then commitment. Love is not an intellectual exercise; it starts in the heart.

Passion that does not lead to commitment has little chance of long term survival. Desire, and even interest, can be fickle. Find those directions that excite you enough to make a commitment and follow them. When the emotion begins to fade, the commitment will keep you going.

Caution, commitment without passion, only lasts so long. When the passion fades, and your commitment is all that is keeping you moving, it is important to rekindle the flame that started the whole process. Feelings follow actions. Start doing the things you did when the passion was new, and the feelings will usually return.

Remember a relationship that failed. We all have them. At some point, we stopped doing the little things that came so naturally in the early stages. We stop sending flowers or making calls. We stop spending time together. We stop "tending the fire."

When your interests and values are in harmony, you have passion. Blind chasing of interests or desires not guided by values and convictions, is lust, and lust leads to certain failure and destruction. Follow those interests that excite you and are supported by your values; opportunities will come from sources beyond your expectations, and success with satisfaction will be yours.

Passion does more to move us in the right direction than any other motivation. Follow your passion—it leads you toward your dream.

TALENTS

What are you good at? Do some things come naturally while others are a struggle? What are your gifts?

We do best that which comes naturally or with which we have some ability. It is true that desire and passion can compensate for a lack of talent, but when desire and talent combine, they are formidable.

I spent much of my life as a sales person with varying degrees of success. As a sales person, I am average, not a superstar. My talents lie in communicating, especially as a speaker. As these abilities have been matched by desire, they have produced more success than I ever realized in sales.

Fortunately, what we are good at is often what we like. Seek out that combination for the best success in life.

MAKE IT HAPPEN; FOLLOW YOUR PASSION

"Faith is the substance of things
hoped for, the evidence of things not
seen." —Hebrews 11:1 (KJV)

Put in everyday terms, "If you believe it, you have to act it." Faith is at the core of "Let it be hot."—Not faith as Kierkegaard described it, a blind irrational leap, but faith that puts action to its convictions.

Picture someone at the airport explaining passionately how safe flight is, the physics of why it works, and encouraging others to get on board. Yet, when it is time to board his own flight, he balks and says he would rather take the bus. Faith in flying means you get on the plane. Faith in life means you act, not talk.

Faith is not platitudes; it is action in a direction. The right direction brings the right destination. Act as if the values you hold are true; if you doubt them, find ones that you can hold true. Act as if you have value; if you doubt your value, remind yourself that you are the product of God's planning. Follow your interests and talents.

(Values + Self Esteem + Direction) × Faith = PASSION

Passion gives life, enthusiasm, and satisfaction.
Passion gives the strength to control your attitude.
Passion is the source you draw on to "LET IT BE HOT!!"

LET IT BE HOT, THE LIFE

A final thought on life. Life is pretty much what you make of it. Make the commitment to live life to the fullest. Be a player, not a spectator.

On a recent trip to England, I rode on a train from Oxford to Wolverhampton. It was the day of a big soccer match (football there) between Crystal of London and the Wolverhampton Wolves. The winner would win the division that year.

Sitting across from me was a man wearing a "team jersey" from Crystal on his way to the match. He was talking loudly, to anyone who would listen, about the match and about other matches he had seen. When he found a listening ear, he described past matches all over England. His refrain was, "I watched... I watched... I watched..."

The thought that overcame my mind was, "I do not want to live this life and say, 'I watched.' I want to be a participant." The greatest loss would be to lie on my deathbed and say, "I wish I had tried."

Our life on this earth is short. We will all leave it someday. Along the way, we are obligated to live life to the fullest. The right direction brings the right destination. How we live each day determines the quality of life we will have, and the ultimate end. Jack London said, "I would rather die in a blaze of glory, than to end my life like dry rot."